BEN & JERRY ... THE REAL SCOOP!

Jules Older and Lyn Severance and Chapters Publishing are donating 7.5% of their profits from this book to teach non-reading parents and their children to read.

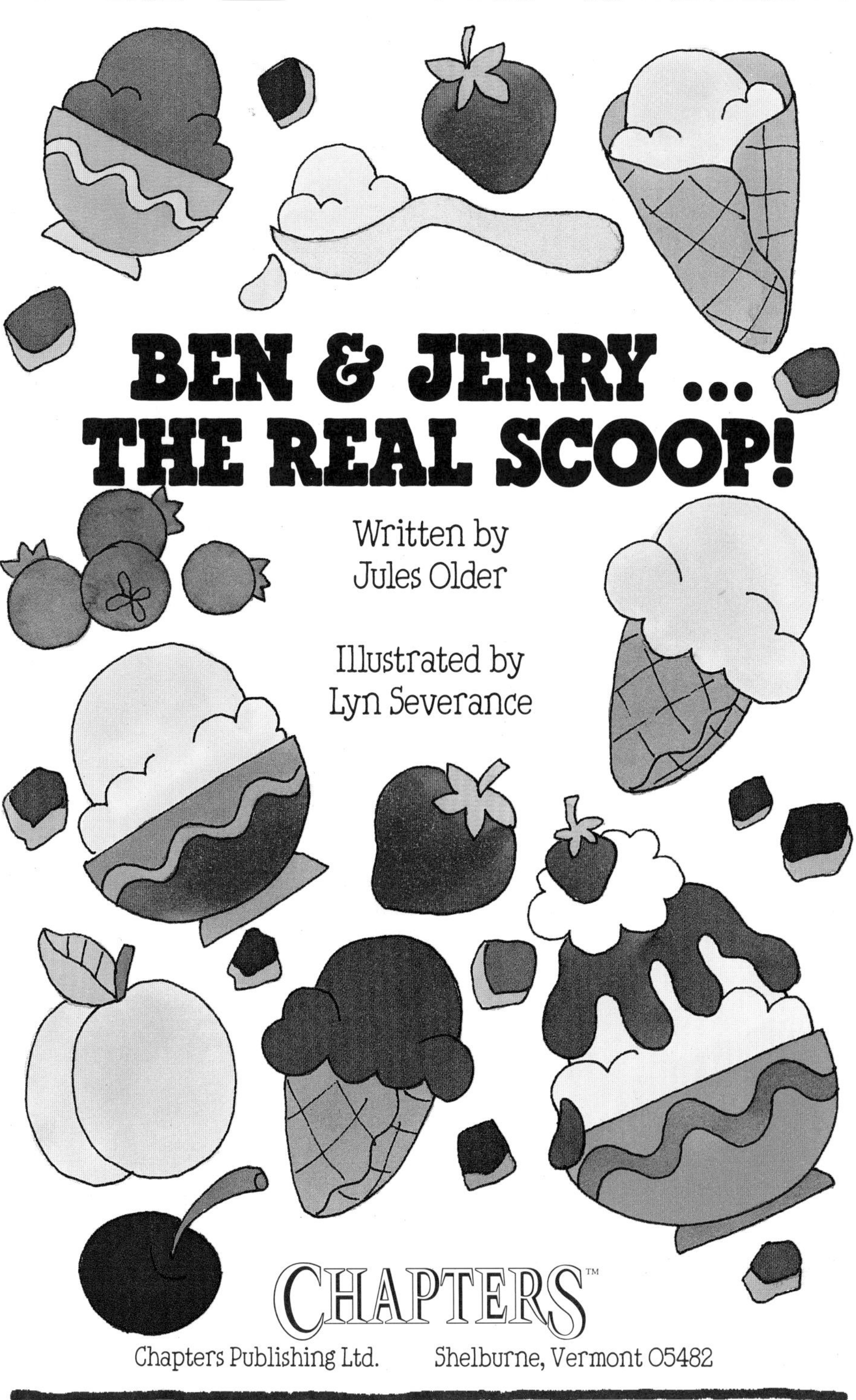

BEN & JERRY ... THE REAL SCOOP!

Written by
Jules Older

Illustrated by
Lyn Severance

CHAPTERS™

Chapters Publishing Ltd. Shelburne, Vermont 05482

To Willow & Amber and Jackson

Published by
Chapters Publishing Ltd.
2031 Shelburne Road
Shelburne, Vermont 05482

Library of Congress Cataloguing-in-Publication Data

Older, Jules.
Ben & Jerry — the real scoop! / written by Jules Older ; illustrated by Lyn Severance.
p. cm.
Summary : A light-hearted look at the background of the two men who founded Ben & Jerry's ice cream company and how their business got started.
ISBN 1-881527-04-2
1. Cohen, Ben (Ben R.)—Juvenile literature. 2. Greenfield, Jerry—Juvenile literature. 3. Businessmen—Vermont—Biography—Juvenile literature. 4. Ben & Jerry's (Firm)—Juvenile literature 5. Ice cream industry—Vermont—Juvenile literature. [1. Cohen, Ben (Ben R.) 2. Greenfield, Jerry. 3. Businessmen. 4. Ben & Jerry's (Firm) 5. Ice cream industry.] I. Severance, Lyn. ill. II. Title.
HD9281.U53V56 1993
338.7'6374--dc20

92-39649
CIP
AC

Trade distribution by
Firefly Books Ltd.
250 Sparks Avenue
Willowdale, Ontario
Canada M2H 2S4

Printed and bound in Canada by
Friesen Printers
Altona, Manitoba

Printed on Eco Matte 50% recycled paper, 10% post consumer waste
The typestyles are Ben & Jerry's Chunk Style and Severance

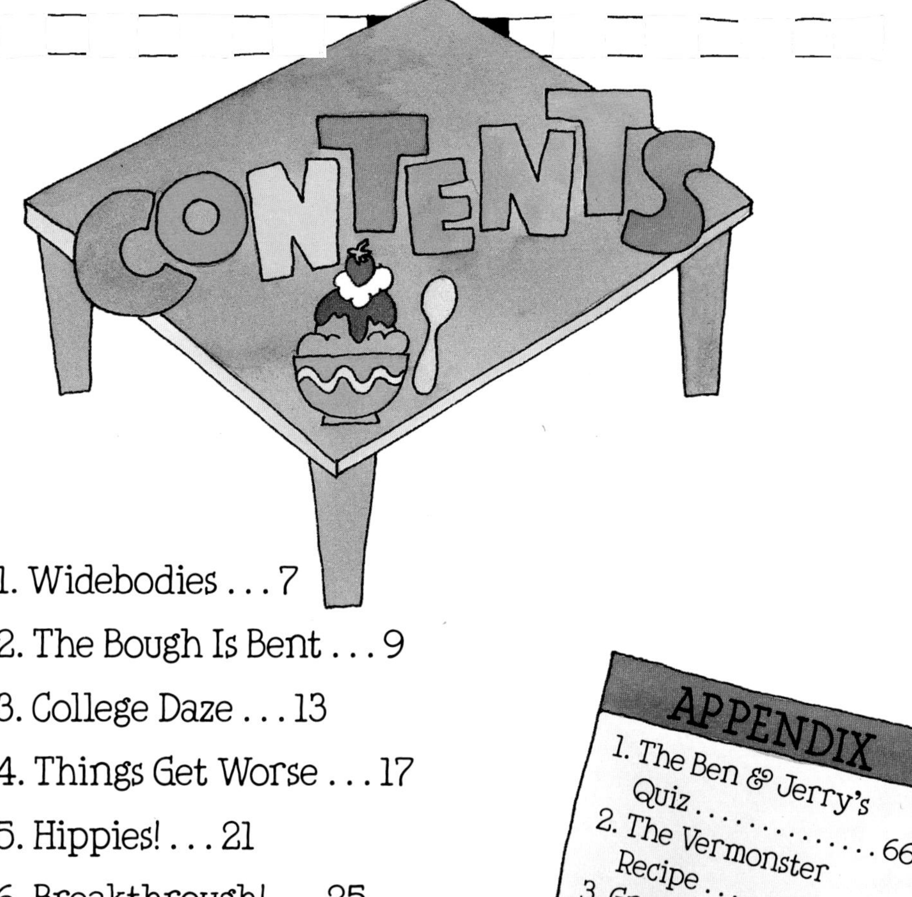

APPENDIX

START HERE!

CHAPTER 1

Widebodies

Once upon a time, in darkest

Long Island, there lived two little widebodies named Jerry and Ben.

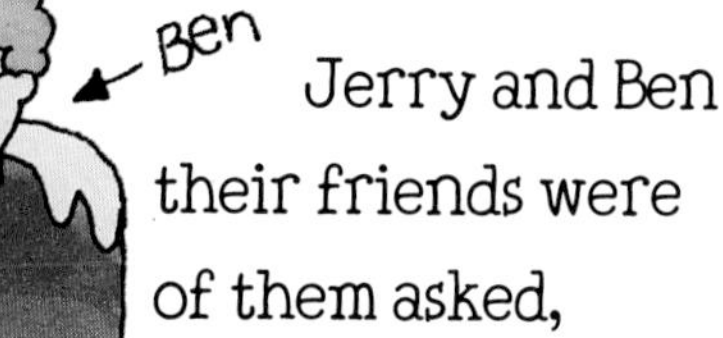

One day, when Jerry and Ben and a bunch of their friends were hanging out, one of them asked, "Whaddaya wanna be when you grow up?"

Lance said, "I wanna be a fireman."

Tiffany said, "I wanna be a fireperson."

Barney said, "I wanna sell men's clothes."

Jerry said, "I wanna be a doctor."

Ben said, "My mom wants me to be a doctor, but I don't think so."

Tiffany asked, "Why not?"

Ben said, "Because I don't like needles, and I hate the smell of doctors' offices."

Jennifer asked, "Then what do you wanna be, Ben?"

Ben rubbed his widebody tummy. "I'll be anything as long as I don't have to run around the school track... and I can eat a little ice cream now and then."

LITTLE DID HE KNOW...

The Bough Is Bent...

Ben sat at the kitchen table watching

his dad devour a half-gallon of chocolate ice cream with a soup spoon.

He looked like a steam shovel at work.

He sounded like this: GLUMPH, GLUMPH, GLUMPH.

Ben's dad (who was something of a widebody himself) said, "And so, Son, as your mother and I were GLUMPH, it's very important that you study hard and go to GLUMPH."

"Sure, Dad."

"If you don't get good grades now, when you apply to college, they'll say, No way, GLUMPH! Ben, are you listening?"

"Yeah, Dad. Why do you keep asking me that?"

"Because you keep staring at my spoon. Now, as I was saying, if you don't get good grades, you'll never get into college, and if you don't get into college, you'll never amount to GLUMPH."

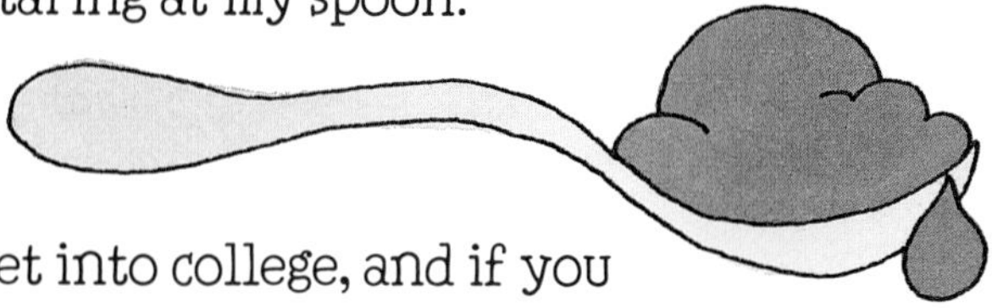

Meanwhile, over at Jerry's house,

Jerry was studying at his little desk. His mother tiptoed into his room. She saw Jerry hard at work, and she smiled a "My Son The Doctor" smile.

She tippy-toed over to Her Son The Almost Doctor. She leaned down, kissed him on the top of his cute little head and said, "That's for being so studious."

From behind her back, she handed him a big bowl of vanilla ice cream. "And this is for my little doctor."

BIG MISTAKE, MOM!

THOUGHTS of CHAIRMEN JERRY & BEN
"If it isn't fun, why do it?"

CHAPTER 3

College Daze

After high school, Jerry &

Ben went separate ways, but they stayed in touch.

Jerry went to Oberlin College in Ohio. His favorite course was called Carnival Techniques.

In Carnival Techniques, Jerry learned to eat fire and break cinderblocks on other people's bellies.

Carnival Techniques is not the kind of course you take to become a doctor.

So, when the time came to apply to medical school (which is where they teach doctors how to give needles and make their offices smell), the medical schools sent Jerry letters that said:

> Dear Jerry,
> Because of an unprecedented number of applications this year, we regret to inform you that you were not among those selected for entry. We wish you the best of blah, blah, blah, blah, blah . . .

This means, "NO WAY, JOSÉ!"

Meanwhile, Ben's college career wasn't exactly blooming.

He went to Colgate (Colgate, the college, not Colgate, the toothpaste). Colgate brushed him off.

He went to Skidmore. Skidmore skidded him out the door.

He passed courses like Jewelry Making 101. You don't become a doctor taking Jewelry Making 101.

Ben didn't become a jewelry maker either. Instead, he quit college and got a job driving an ice cream truck.

For Jerry and Ben, things were not going well.

BUT THINGS WERE ABOUT TO GET WORSE!

THOUGHTS of CHAIRMEN JERRY& BEN
Business has a responsibility to give back to the community from which it gains its support.

CHAPTER 4

Things Get Worse

Our story so far . . .

Jerry and Ben, a couple of Long Island widebodies, are into ice cream but are definitely not into:

1. Running around the track
2. Running around anything
3. Studying physics
4. Studying anything (except for jewelry making and fire eating and cinderblock smashing)
5. Medical school
6. Any school.

How could things possibly get worse?

Here's how . . .

1. Jerry again applied to medical school. Again, he got back letters that said, NO WAY, JOSÉ!
2. Ben quit driving the ice cream truck.
3. Jerry got a job. Jerry's job was mashing up beef livers and stuffing them into test tubes.

This kind of job is called Lab Technician.

This kind of job is gross.

4. Ben got half the jobs on the East Coast. After driving the ice cream truck, he drove a taxi. Then he delivered pottery wheels; then he flipped hamburgers. Next he guarded a racetrack, and finally he went into floor mopping.

Ben mopped the floors of a department store. He mopped the floors of an apartment building. He even mopped the floors of an ice cream store!

5. He was a wonderful floor mopper.

6. But his mother still wanted him to be a doctor!

OY!

THOUGHTS of CHAIRMEN JERRY & BEN
"The more we give away, the better we do."

CHAPTER 5

Hippies

After a while, Jerry got sick of

mashing up beef livers and stuffing them into test tubes. Ben grew weary of mopping.

So Jerry and Ben got together and did what a lot of people who didn't get into medical school and who mopped floors instead of going to college did. They became . . . HIPPIES!

hip•pie (hip´e) n. Also hippy pl. -pies. A member of a loosely knit nonconformist group, esp. one that rejects conventional social mores, accepts universal love, and wants to make the world a groovier place.

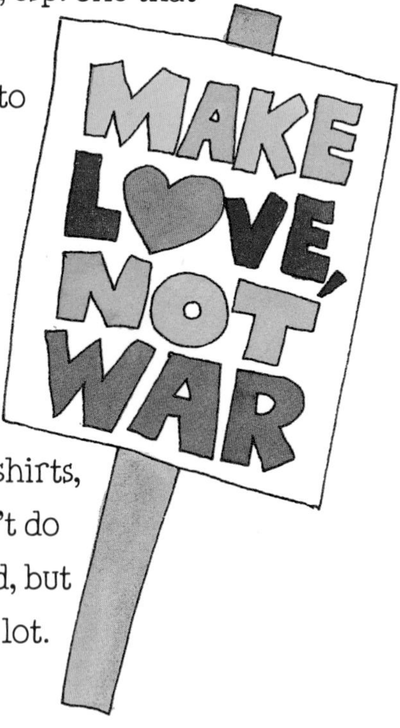

This means that hippies went to Peace Marches carrying signs that read, "Make Love, Not War." They were kind to people and animals. They wore long hair and tie-dyed T-shirts, and they didn't wear ties. They didn't do things just because everybody else did, but they did say "Groovy!" and "Wow!" a lot. Like a whole lot, man.

Can you dig it?

Jerry and Ben could dig it like a whole lot, man.

But they knew that sooner or later, and probably sooner, they would have to eat.

And to eat, sooner or later, and hopefully later, they would have to work.

Ben said, "Whaddaya wanna do, Jer?"

"I dunno. Whadda you wanna do, Ben?"

Ben stared at the sky. "The truth is, Jer, I really wanna do three things."

"What's that, Ben?"

"I want to make a little money. I want to do good things for the world. And I want to have fun."

"Amazing!"

"What's so amazing?"

"It's amazing, Ben, because that's exactly what I wanna do, too! Now all we gotta do is figure out how!"

The two pals thought and thought. They thought until their brains were full and their stomachs were empty.

When their tummy rumbles got too loud for them to think any more, they walked across the street and bought themselves ice cream cones.

Jerry bought vanilla fudge. Ben bought strawberry.

Then they went back to thinking.

WHAT DO YOU THINK THEY THOUGHT ABOUT?

THOUGHTS of CHAIRMEN JERRY & BEN
"Business is a powerful force and can be a powerful force for good."

Breakthrough!

You guessed it — they thought

about ice cream.

They thought about how good that ice cream tasted.

They thought about how much more fun it was to eat ice cream than to mop floors or mash up beef livers.

They thought about how much nicer eating ice cream was than giving—or getting—needles.

They thought about how, if the Fairy Godmother granted them three wishes, the first two would involve ice cream.

Then Ben said, "Yeah, but whaddaya wanna do, Jer?"

And Jerry shouted, "BREAKTHROUGH!"

Ben looked at his pal the way you look at somebody when you've said, "Nice day, isn't it?" and they scream, "EASTER BUNNY!"

"Uh, whaddaya mean, 'Breakthrough,' Jer?"

"I mean . . . I mean . . . Ben, look at me. What are we doing?"

"Sitting here trying to figure out how to make a little money."

"And what else are we doing?"

"Eating ice cream."

"Exactly."

"Yeah, but what does—?"

"Don't you see? That's how we'll make money!"

"Eating ice cream? Jerry, nobody will pay us to eat—"

"No, man—we're not just gonna eat ice cream. Man, we're gonna make ice cream! Can you dig it?"

Ben sat and thought. He licked his ice cream cone. The strawberry tasted good. He licked some more. He thought some more.

Slowly, slowly, ever-so-slowly, a little smile crept onto Ben's face.

The smile grew into a grin.

The grin grew into a laugh.

The laugh grew into a great big, ear-to-ear, shoulder-shaking, thigh slapping, nose-snorting, tears-in-your-eyes, choke-on-your-sugar-cone, hee-haw hee-haw, widebelly laugh.

Ben clapped Jerry on the back and yelled,

THOUGHTS of CHAIRMEN JERRY & BEN
"Never trust a skinny ice cream maker!"

CHAPTER 7

Jerry & Ben's Ice Cream

But one thing was wrong.

Jerry didn't know diddly about making ice cream.

Ben didn't know squat.

But they knew how to learn. They sent five whole dollars off to Pennsylvania for a course in How to Make Ice Cream. It was something like Carnival Techniques, only eating ice cream was a lot cooler than eating fire.

Then they had to decide where they wanted to make their ice cream.

Ben said, "I like Burlington, Vermont. It's full of students, and not one ice cream shop."

Jerry looked at him funny. "Ben, it's cold in Vermont. Do students eat ice cream when it's snowing?"

Ben smiled. "We do. Let's hope Vermonters will, too."

So they moved to Vermont. They rented a little house on a little island in Lake Champlain. They started making ice cream in a little ice cream maker in their little living room.

Where do you think they got the ice to freeze the cream? They chopped it out of Lake Champlain. (Jerry was right about Vermont being cold.)

Jerry and Ben invented new flavors. Some of them worked. Like Heath Bar Crunch. Some of them didn't. Like Lemon Peppermint Carob Chip.

Some were great. Like New York Super Fudge Chunk. Some were awful. Like the flavor that tasted like garlic, bounced like a ball and stretched like Plastic Man. Jerry and Ben ate it anyway, but none of their friends would.

As Jerry and Ben tested new flavors, they made a discovery. They discovered that they were getting rounder and more widebellied every day.

You could say they grew with the job.

They knew that if they wanted to weigh less than a couple of sperm whales, they would to have to get other people to eat up their ice cream.

So they rented a broken-down gas station.

It had holes in the roof.

And holes in the walls.

And holes in the floor.

And holes in the holes. (It was really broken down.)

They filled the holes and swept out the cobwebs and cleaned the walls, and they were just getting ready to paint a sign for over the door that said JERRY & BEN'S ICE CREAM...

when

Ben

said,

"Uh, Jer . . . "

"Yes, Ben?"

"Uh, Jer . . ."

he

said

again.

"Yes, Ben?"

Ben took a deep breath. "Uh, Jer, Idon'tthinkJERRY&BEN'Ssoundsasniceas . . . as . . . as . . . "

"Yes, Ben?"

"As, well er um uh as . . . BEN & JERRY'S."

"Yes, Ben."

"You mean it, Jer? BEN & JERRY'S—you can dig it?"

"I can dig it."

"Like wow! We'll call it BEN & JERRY'S. BEN & JERRY'S HOMEMADE. And because your name comes second, you can be President!"

"And because your name comes first, Ben, I hereby anoint you Vice President. Ta da!"

As President Jerry and Vice President Ben painted the sign to go over the gas station door, little did they know that they were about to
have a . . .

FOOD FIGHT!

THOUGHTS of CHAIRMEN JERRY & BEN
We make the only super-premium ice cream whose name you can pronounce.

CHAPTER 8

Food Fight!

Vice President: Hey, Jer,

what's with this batch of chocolate chip ice cream?

President: Isn't it great? I love it.

Vice President: I hate it.

President: You hate it? How come?

Vice President: What do you call these things, Jerry? These tiny little itty-bitty things.

President: I call 'em chocolate chips, Ben. What do you call 'em?

Vice President: Chocolate flecks. Chocolate specks. Chocolate freckles. Jerry, those chips are so small, you need a microscope to see them.

President: Oh yeah?

Vice President: Oh yeah! And nothing bigger than an ant could taste 'em!

President: Oh yeah?

Vice President: Oh yeah! I like big chunks of chocolate. BIG chunks!

President: Look, Ben, we've been over this before. If you make the chunks too big, some spoonfuls aren't going to have any chunks at all. And I HATE a spoonful without any chunks.

Vice President: Oh yeah?

President: Oh yeah!

Vice President: But if you make ‘em too small, you won’t be able to taste the chocolate at all. And I HATE tasteless ice cream.

President: Hmmm . . .

Vice President: Hmmm . . .

Together: BREAKTHROUGH!

President: If we make the chunks big—

Vice President: And we put in a whole lot of ’em—

Together:
THERE’LL BE BIG CHUNKS IN EVERY SPOONFUL!

THOUGHTS of CHAIRMEN JERRY & BEN
"Our success is a shock to us. And quite frankly, it's a shock to anyone who knows us."

CHAPTER 9

What's Going On?

Our story so far... Ben and

Jerry left Long Island, left college(s), left their jobs and moved to Vermont. In a little house on a little island, they tested new flavors and grew stomachs as big as North Carolina. They fixed up an old gas station, hung a sign over the door and found a peaceful solution to their food fight.

As we join them now, the two pals are just about to . . . OPEN FOR BUSINESS.

OPEN

"Well, Ben, old pal, we've swept the floor, painted the sign and made the ice cream. I sure hope somebody comes."

"Jerry, old buddy, trust me—they'll come. Who can say no to ice cream with big chunks and lots of 'em?"

"Yeah, but we've been open almost three minutes, and nobody's walked in yet. How are people gonna' know about those big chunks?"

"Don't worry, I've got it all figured out. If we can't sell our ice cream, we'll just . . . give it away!"

"Give it away? Ben, sometimes I worry about you. I wish you'd gone to business school."

But people did come to the old gas station with the BEN & JERRY'S HOMEMADE sign over the door. First a few came, then a few more, then a lot more, and soon there were long lines outside waiting for a scoop of Ben & Jerry's Homemade ice cream. They came in spring, in summer, in fall and, yes, even in the snow. (Ben was right about the Vermonters.)

The reason people kept coming was that the ice cream tasted so good. And *that's* because it's made from natural flavors and real cream. It's a lot heavier than most ice cream because it has a lot more goodies and a lot less air. It's heavy stuff, man!

The guys were scooping faster than a couple of bailers in a leaky boat. They scooped all day and made ice cream all night. But no matter how much they made, they couldn't make enough. The lines outside got longer. And longer.

A n d lonnnnnger.

Soon Ben and Jerry had to hire people to help scoop ice cream. Then they had to hire more people to help make ice cream.

And still they couldn't keep the ice cream coming fast enough. Day and night, night and day, all they could think about was ice cream.

Then, one morning, Ben said, "Whoa!"

Jerry said, "Whoa? Whaddaya mean, 'whoa'? We're just barely keeping up now. Pass the French Vanilla."

"I'm sayin', whoa! and I mean, whoa! Jer, we started this to do three things, right? I'm out of French Vanilla.

"Right. To make a little money . . . "

"To do good things for the world . . . "

"And to have fun. Ben, I'm running low on Maple Walnut."

"Listen, Jer, we're making money—here's the Maple—but we gotta do more good—"

"You're right. And have more fun, too. Now all we have to do is figure out how."

Ben yelled, "I CAN'T FIGURE OUT ANYTHING IF I'M SCOOPING ICE CREAM ALL THE TIME!"

Jerry whispered, "Oh."

So the guys stopped scooping ice cream.

They closed the gas station door.

They pulled down the shades. They put up a sign.

The sign said,

WE'RE CLOSED BECAUSE WE'RE TRYING TO FIGURE OUT WHAT'S GOING ON.

CHAPTER 10

Freebies!

The two guys figured & figured

While they were figuring, they tried a taste of Heath Bar Crunch and a smidgen of New York Super Fudge Chunk. Eating ice cream always improved the quality of their thinking.

Jerry said, "Ok, we've got three things here—making a little money, doing good and having fun. The money's OK. That leaves doing good and (lick) having fun."

Ben sighed. "Yeah, but which one (lick) do we tackle first?"

Then they both shouted, "BREAKTHROUGH! Let's do 'em (double lick) together!"

So. How do you do good and have fun at the same time?

Well, if you happen to own an ice cream factory, it isn't that hard. Start by . . . giving away ice cream!

And that's just what the two guys did.

In May, they held a Mother's Day Giveaway and gave one free cone to every woman. Two cones to every pregnant woman. (Can you guess why?)

In August, they held a Dog Days Giveaway and gave one free scoop to every pooch.

In October, they held a Fall Down and made the world's biggest bagel!

They did something else at Fall Down, too. They built a stage.

A gang of really strong guys carried Ben onto the stage. He was wearing a white turban and a white towel—a very big white towel.

The announcer said, "Introducing the famous Indian swami, Habeeni Ben Coheeni!" Ben smiled a swami smile.

Then Jerry marched onto the stage.

He was wearing a pith helmet.

He was carrying a sledgehammer.

He didn't smile at all.

The really strong guys laid Ben across two chairs and put a cinderblock right in the middle of his really round widebelly.

Jerry stared at Ben.

He stared at the crowd.

He stared at the cinderblock.

He raised his sledgehammer.

Higher.

And Higher.

And (gulp) HIGHER!

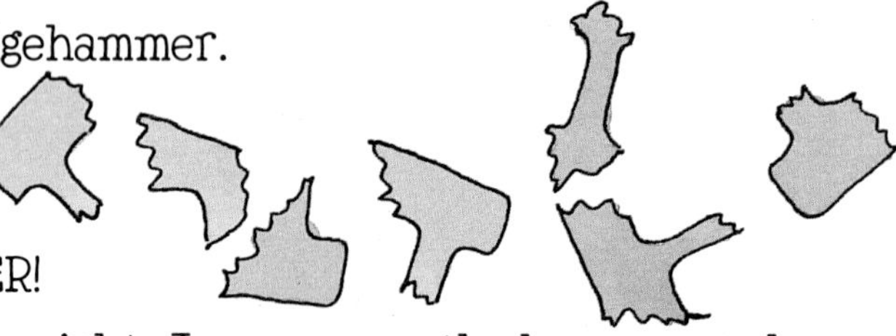

Then, with all his might, Jerry swung the hammer and smashed the cinderblock! The cinderblock broke into a thousand little cinders and a million little blocks. And Ben wasn't even hurt.

"Carnival Techniques" had finally paid off.

After Fall Down, Ben and Jerry drove a big truck to St. Albans, Vermont. People in St. Albans were feeling sad because the railroad shops had closed, and there wasn't much work.

Ben and Jerry decided to cheer them up. They backed the truck up to a big plastic swimming pool. Right in the pool (which was conveniently empty at the time), they made the world's biggest ice cream sundae.

When they finished making the world's biggest sundae, everybody in St. Albans pulled out their spoons . . . and dove in!

In case you want to make one, here's the recipe:

TAKE 20,421 POUNDS OF VANILLA, CHOCOLATE AND MINT ICE CREAM. ADD 300 POUNDS OF LIQUID CHOCOLATE, AND 300 POUNDS OF CHOCOLATE CHIPS. POUR ON 1,381 POUNDS OF VERMONT MAPLE SYRUP, AND 300 POUNDS OF CHERRIES, AND 300 POUNDS OF STRAWBERRIES, AND 1,500 POUNDS OF PEACHES, AND 2,000 POUNDS OF PINEAPPLES. SPRINKLE ON 100 POUNDS OF WALNUTS, AND 100 POUNDS OF PISTACHIOS, AND 100 POUNDS OF PEANUTS. TOP WITH 300 POUNDS OF WHIPPED CREAM. TA DA!
DIVE IN!

Ben and Jerry gave away ice cream because they wanted to do good and have fun.

But when you give away stuff, people talk about it.

When you smash cinderblocks on somebody's belly, people talk about it.

When you build an ice cream sundae in a swimming pool, people talk about it.

And when you make ice cream worth standing in line for, people talk about it.

Before long, everybody in Vermont was talking about Ben & Jerry.

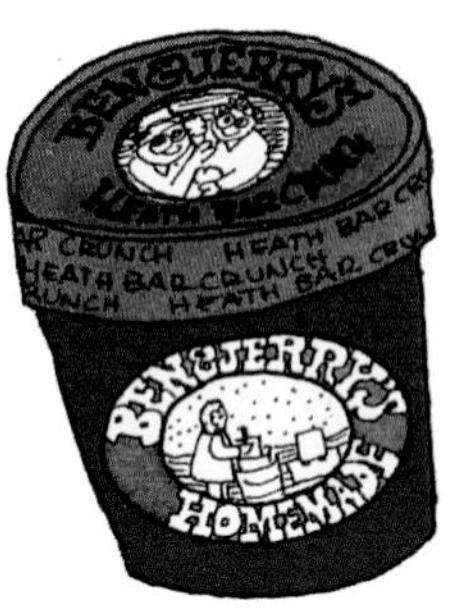

And pretty soon restaurants heard about the ice cream with big chunks and lots of 'em. They put Ben & Jerry's on their menus.

Then stores heard about the ice cream with big chunks and lots of 'em. They put Ben & Jerry's in their freezers.

Then a giant food company heard about the ice cream with big chunks and lots of 'em. They put Ben & Jerry's in the hands of their lawyers.

That could only mean one thing—

T.R.O.U.B.L.E!

CHAPTER 11

T.R.O.U.B.L.E.

The giant company was

called Pillsbury. Pillsbury's ads featured a cute little fat guy called the Doughboy.

Pillsbury made an ice cream they named Häagen-Dazs. (It was hard to pronounce, but they sold a lot of it.) Pillsbury told the storekeepers, "Look here, buddy—if you sell this Ben & Whazisname's ice cream, you can't sell Häagen-Dazs. So get rid of the widebodies, ok?"

Sorry, Guys

The storekeepers told Ben and Jerry, "Sorry, guys. We love the big chunks, but we don't want trouble with Pillsbury. We can't sell your ice cream."

"That nerdy little Doughboy can't do this to us!" Ben shouted.

"He just did," Jerry sighed.

"Are we gonna take it lying down?"

"Let's sleep on it."

"Are we men or mice?"

"Were you squeaking to me?"

"C'mon, Jer—we've got to fight back!"

WHAT'S THE DOUGH BOY AFRAID OF?
BEN & JERRY'S

Ah, but how do you fight back when you're just two real guys from Vermont, and you're up against a giant corporation with busloads of lawyers at their international headquarters in Minneapolis?

"You're right, Ben. They can't do this to us. We're fighting back, starting now. I'm outa here!"

"Where are you going, Jer?"

"Minneapolis!"

Jerry flew to Pillsbury Headquarters in Minneapolis carrying a picket sign. The sign said, "What's the Doughboy Afraid Of?"

Jerry walked back and forth in front of the giant Pillsbury building. Newspaper reporters wrote articles about him, and photographers took pictures of his sign.

Back in Vermont, Ben and the rest of the gang made "What's the Doughboy Afraid Of?" bumper stickers. And "What's the Doughboy Afraid Of?" T-shirts. And "What's the Doughboy Afraid Of?" signs to put on buses.

"Now we're havin' fun," he chuckled. "Let's see what we can do next."

Here's what they did next: they put an ad in "Rolling Stone" magazine. The ad said, "Help two Vermont hippies battle the giant Pillsbury Corporation."

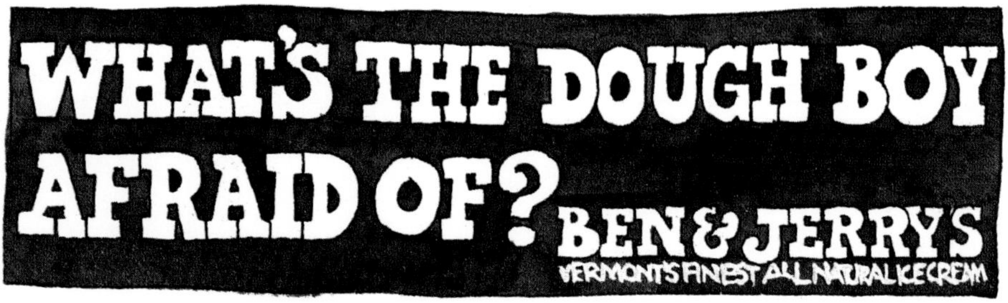

And you know what? People did. They wrote to Pillsbury. They said things like:

"Hey bigshot, what's the Doughboy afraid of, huh? Huh? Huh?"

And,

"Unless you learn to co-exist peacefully with your competitor, I am never, ever going to purchase any product you make, period. Never, ever again. Is that understood?"

And,

"Get your piggy paws off Ben and Jerry, you big, blown-up bullfrog!"

After a few thousand phone calls, Pillsbury made a call of its own.

Pillsbury called Vermont and said, "Well, boys, you've made your point. Maybe there's room for both of us in the freezer."

And you know what?

THERE WAS!

CHAPTER 12

Good News & Bad News

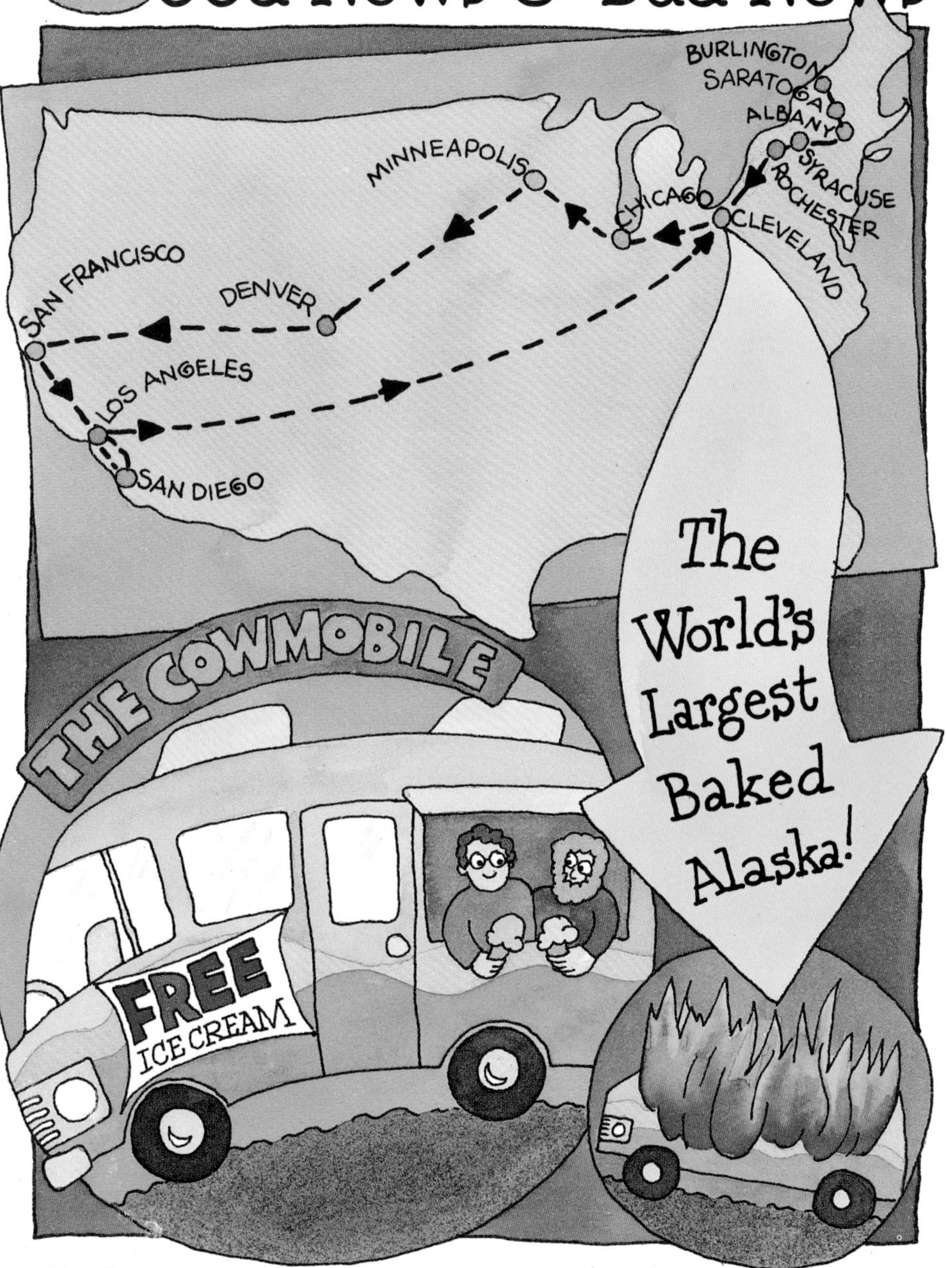

After they won the fight with

the Doughboy, Ben and Jerry decided it was time to let the rest of the country try their ice cream.

But the rest of the country had never heard of Ben & Jerry's.

If you made ice cream in, say, Vermont and wanted people in, say, California to try it, how would you let them know how good it tastes?

Most companies would put a lot of ads on television.

But Ben & Jerry's isn't most companies. They bought an old van, painted it with cows and green fields and fluffy clouds, and filled it full of freezers.

They filled the freezers full of ice cream.

They named the van, "Cowmobile."

Then they drove Cowmobile s-l-o-w-l-y across the United States, from Vermont to California, giving out free ice cream along the way.

When they reached California, they turned Cowmobile over to Liz and Halsey, who scooped ice cream for Ben & Jerry's . . . and who had just gotten married.

Ben and Jerry said good-bye to California, good-bye to Cowmobile and good-bye to Liz and Halsey. Then they flew back to Vermont.

One day, their phone rang . . .

"I have a collect call from Liz for Ben or Jerry. Will you accept the charges?"

"Sure. Hi, Liz, this is Jerry. Where are you?"

"Hi, Jerry. Just outside Cleveland."

"How's the trip going?"

"That's why I'm calling. I've got good news and bad news."

"Tell me the good news first, Liz."

"OK, the good news is that we've driven Cowmobile from California to Ohio, giving out free ice cream the whole way. People love it! Pretty soon we'll be a national company."

"Liz, that's wonderful. So what's the bad news?"

"Are you sitting or standing?"

"Standing."

"Sit."

"OK, I'm sitting."

"The bad news is that about five minutes ago, Cowmobile caught fire."

"Oh, no!"

"Oh, yes! And right now it's burning to the ground in the middle of a Cleveland parking lot."

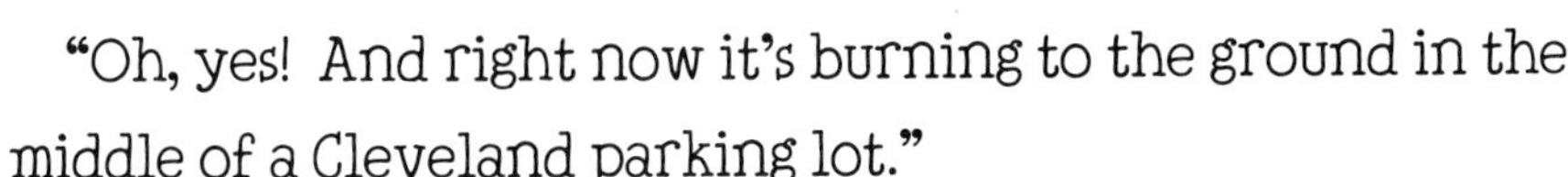

"Liz, that's terrible."

"Yeah, but it's not all terrible."

"What do you mean?"

"Well, with all that ice cream in the freezers, Jerry, we've just created the world's biggest Baked Alaska! Call the Guinness Book of World Records—we'll be famous!"

Can two guys from Long Island find happiness as ice cream makers in Vermont? And can they make a little money, do good and have fun while they're at it?

READ THE LAST CHAPTER . . . AND FIND OUT!

CHAPTER 13

The Last Chapter

DOING W__L BY DOING G__D!

Ben and Jerry wanted to make

great ice cream, and while they were at it, make a little money, do good things for the world and have fun. Let's see how they're doing...

1. DO THEY MAKE GREAT ICE CREAM?

Do they make great ice cream! One taste and you'll know what the Doughboy was afraid of.

2. DO THEY MAKE A LITTLE MONEY?

No, they don't.

They make a whole lot of money. They make a lot of money because so many folks buy their great ice cream.

3. ARE THEY DOING GOOD THINGS FOR THE WORLD?

Every time Ben & Jerry's makes a dollar, they give seven-and-a-half cents to people who need money to do more good things. F'rinstance...

Ben & Jerry's gives money to the Devastators, an all-kids band that plays for peace and justice.

They give money to the Heifer Project, a farmer's group that gives cows and goats to poor people so they can feed themselves with milk and cheese.

And they give a lot of money to the Vermont Children's Forum, a group of adults that make sure good things happen for kids.

Peace and ice cream go together like Batman and Robin. Like Lois Lane and Superman. Like Ben and Jerry.

And that's not all. They buy the stuff that goes into their ice cream from people who really need the money. They buy: peaches from Black family farmers,

blueberries from Maine Indians,

and brownies from a bakery that works with poor people in Yonkers, New York.

When the price of milk dropped, some Vermont dairy farmers almost lost their farms. Ben & Jerry's paid them extra money for their milk—and tried to get other ice cream companies to pay more, too.

But maybe Ben & Jerry's best adventure in doing good came when they helped save the Brazilian rainforest.

One day, Ben said, "This is terrible!"

"What's terrible, Ben?"

"Some people in Brazil are cutting down the rainforest. The families who live in the forest need those trees to gather Brazil nuts. And the whole world needs those trees to help keep our air clean. Boy, I wish we could help!"

"Yeah, but how can an ice cream company in Vermont help save a forest in Brazil?"

"Let's get some ice cream and think about it."

The guys got out two pints of ice cream and two soup spoons. Jerry chose New York Super Fudge Chunk. Ben chose Chunky Monkey.

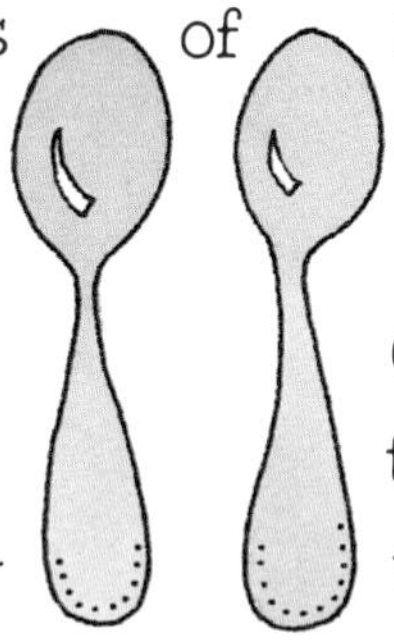

Ben said, "The trouble is GLUMPH the trees are worth more for lumber than for nuts. That's why people keep cutting them down."

Jerry said, "So if the nuts were worth more than the lumber, people GLUMPH would stop cutting them down."

And together they shouted, "BREAKGLUMPH!"

Ben said, "We'll buy the nuts—"

Jerry said, "— and use them in a new flavor of ice cream. We'll call it . . . Brazilian Bounce!"

"Nah, Jer, it sounds like one of our failure flavors. What about . . . Nutty Nougat?"

"Nah, Ben, that sounds like it would pull out all your fillings."

They both ate some more ice cream.

Then, suddenly and without warning, they shouted, "RAINFOREST CRUNCH!"

So Ben & Jerry's started buying Brazil nuts and making Rainforest Crunch.

And that's how an ice cream company in Vermont can help save a forest in Brazil.

4. YEAH, BUT ARE THEY HAVING FUN?

Here are some facts. Decide for yourself . . .

- Everybody who works at Ben & Jerry's gets three free pints of ice cream a day.
- They also get free time at a health club to work off those three pints at night.
- Every Friday, everybody gets free cookies, too. BIG cookies with LOTS of chocolate chips.
- They also get free backrubs. And footrubs.
- And nobody has to wear a suit. Or a tie. Especially, a tie. Ever.
- The guys still give away a lot of ice cream. When Vermont turned 200 years old, Ben & Jerry's sent an ice cream truck to every town in the state. The truck was full of free ice cream.

Happy birthday, Vermont!
Love,
Ben and Jer

- Then they sent Ben & Jerry's Circus Bus around the whole country. A free show and ice cream, too!
- And every year they throw big music parties for lots and lots of people.

Does this sound like fun to you?

IT'S FUN TO THEM!

The Last-Last Chapter

Jerry wanted to be a doctor,

and Ben's mom wanted him to be a doctor, too. Instead, they came to Vermont and made ice cream.

But one beautiful Saturday morning in May, the University of Vermont made Ben and Jerry honorary doctors of law.

So on Monday, when they went to work, Ben and Jerry could tell everybody to call them "Doctor Ben" and "Doctor Jerry."

They could . . .

BUT THEY DIDN'T.

THE • END

BEN&JERRY'S QUIZ

Q: What happened to the old gas station where Ben and Jerry started selling ice cream?

A: It's in Service Station Heaven. But Ben and Jerry saved all the old signs, and they've got them stored away somewhere. Maybe someday they'll remember where.

GAS

GAS

WELCOME TO SERVICE STATION HEAVEN

Q: Who made most of the signs?

A: The same person who drew the pictures for this book: Lyn Severance.

Q: Ben & Jerry's now has three ice cream factories in Vermont. One's in Waterbury . . . Where are the other two?

A: Let's see . . . Waterbury opened in 1985. In 1988 they started making ice cream in Springfield, and in 1994, a brand-new ice cream factory will bring the big chill to St. Albans. (Yes, the same St. Albans where the guys made that 27,102-pound ice cream sundae.)

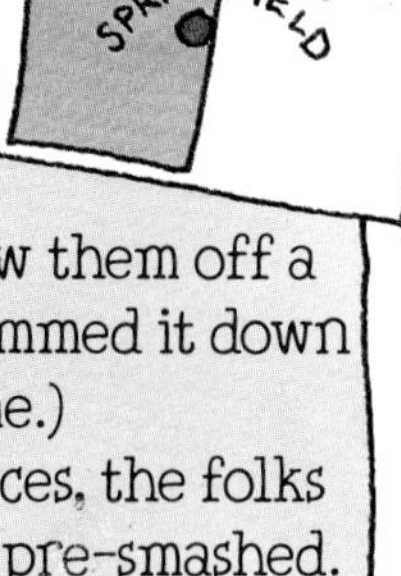

ST. ALBANS

WATERBURY

SPRINGFIELD

Q: How do they break up Heath® Bars for Heath Bar Crunch?

A: At first, Jerry cut them into pieces with a knife. Then he smashed them with a hammer. Then he threw them off a ladder. Then he took the whole box and slammed it down on the concrete floor. (Don't try this at home.)

Nowadays, Ben & Jerry's uses so many pieces, the folks at Heath send them to the ice cream factory pre-smashed.

Q: Speaking of nuts (and beans), what five chunks can you taste in New York Super Fudge Chunk?
A: If your taste buds are in 1 good shape, you can taste 2 pecans, 3 walnuts, chocolate-covered almonds, 4 dark chocolate & 5 white chocolate. If your taste buds aren't in good shape, put them on a strict program of daily exercise right away!
Q: What's the all-time most popular flavor?
A: The envelope, please. And the winner is (long drum roll) . . . Heath Bar Crunch!
Q: Ok, what's the second most popular flavor?
A: Ladies and Gentlemen, the number-two favorite is (short drum roll) . . . New York Super Fudge Chunk!
Q: Speaking of crunch, what nuts go into making Rainforest Crunch?
A: Brazil nuts and cashews.
Q: Well then, what's the fastest growing flavor?
A: Setting new records for rapid rising is . . . Chocolate Chip Cookie Dough!
Q: How many cows give their milk to make Ben & Jerry's ice cream?
A: Moo-re than 23,000. And that's no bull.

Q: How many farmers milk those cows?

A: The milk comes from more than 528 family farms.

Q: How much money does Ben & Jerry's give away every year to help kids and families?

A: They give seven and a half cents out of every dollar they make.

Q: How much money from this book is being given away to help a good cause?

A: Same as Ben & Jerry's. Seven and a half cents from every dollar. The good cause is the Vermont Reading Project, which helps moms and dads teach their k-i-d-s to r-e-a-d.

Q: How much ice cream does Ben & Jerry's give away to help good causes?

A: A wicked lot of ice cream. A wicked lot!

BONUS QUESTION
Q: What was the first flavor that Ben & Jerry's sold?
A: Believe it or not, their first flavor was plain old vanilla.
DOUBLE BONUS QUESTION
Q: All right, what was the first flavor they invented?
A: Oreo® Mint, which was later changed to Mint with Oreo Cookies, which was even later changed to Mint Chocolate Cookie.
THE LAST QUESTION
Q: Who's older, Ben or Jer?
A: Well, Ben was born on March 18, 1951. Jerry was born on March 14. Let's see . . . that makes him—yes!—four days older.
MARCH
S M T W Th F S
THE LAST, LAST QUESTION
Q: Who was the flavor Cherry Garcia named after?
A: Ask your mom or dad.
THE END

HOW TO MAKE A VERM

The Vermonster is the biggest concoction that you can make without a swimming pool. You can create one at home—but unless you work fast, you'll end up with multi-flavor mush!

- 20 scoops of ice cream, any combination of flavors
- 4 bananas, sliced
- 1 Brownie, broken into pieces
- 3 giant chocolate-chip cookies, broken into pieces
- 1 cup coarsely chopped walnuts
- 1 small chocolate bar, coarsely chopped
- 1 small pack Reese's Pieces
- 1 small pack plain chocolate M&M's
- 1/2 cup hot fudge sauce
- 1/2 cup of whipped cream
- 8 fresh strawberries, cut in half

GREAT M
ICE CREA

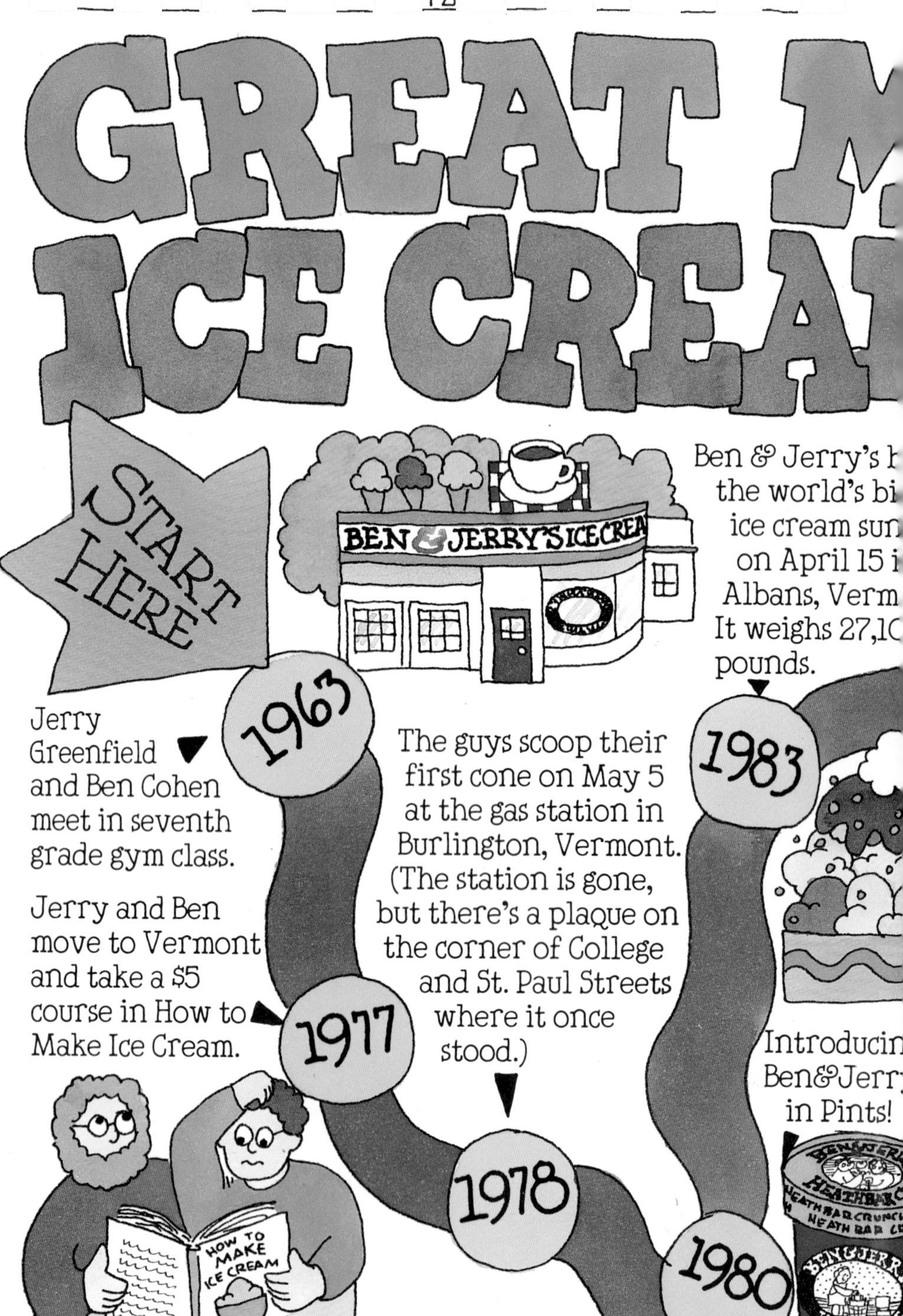

Ben & Jerry's h
the world's bi
ice cream sun
on April 15 i
Albans, Verm
It weighs 27,10
pounds.

Jerry Greenfield and Ben Cohen meet in seventh grade gym class.

Jerry and Ben move to Vermont and take a $5 course in How to Make Ice Cream.

The guys scoop their first cone on May 5 at the gas station in Burlington, Vermont. (The station is gone, but there's a plaque on the corner of College and St. Paul Streets where it once stood.)

Introducin
Ben&Jerr
in Pints!

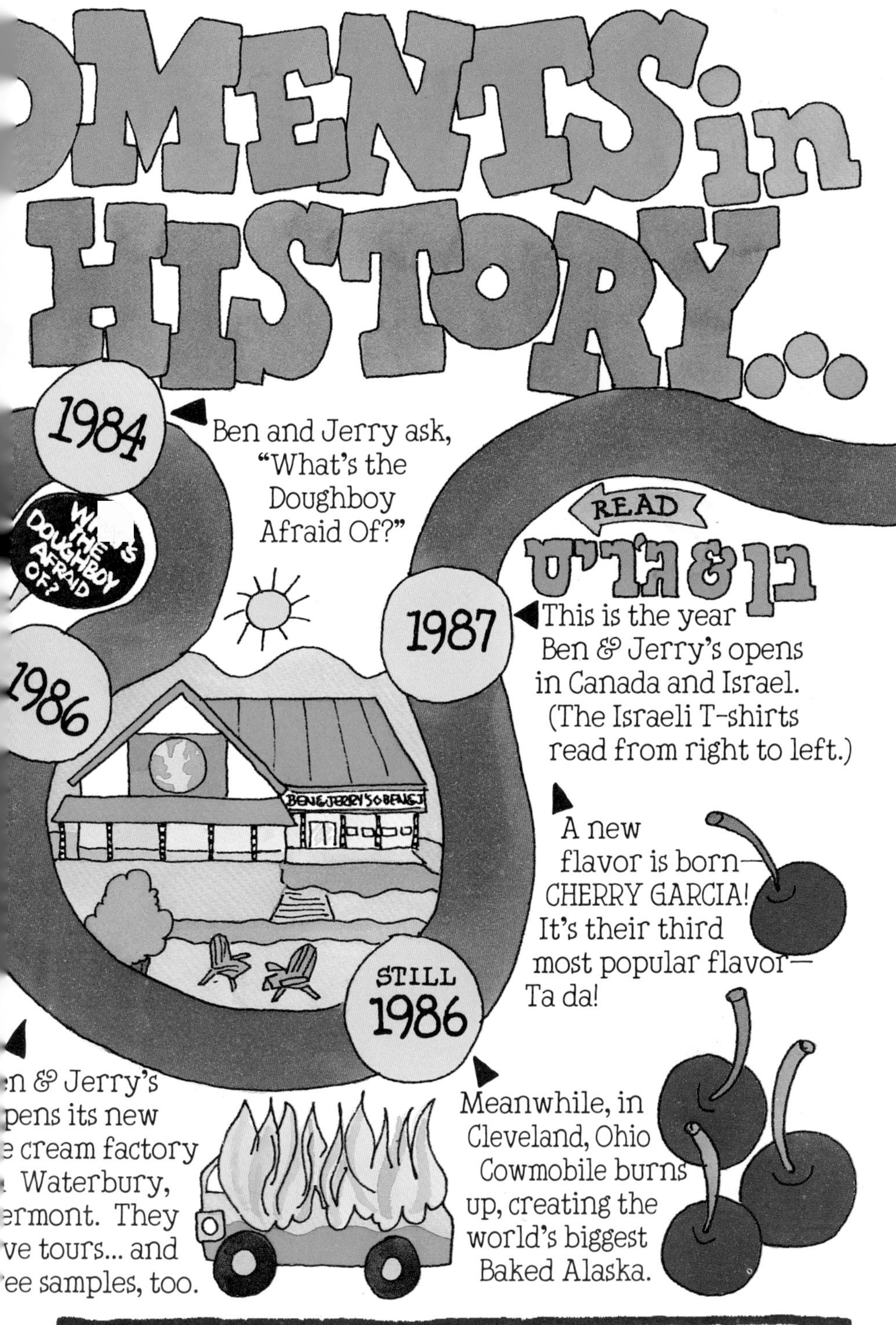
MENTS in
HISTORY...
1984
Ben and Jerry ask, "What's the Doughboy Afraid Of?"
DOUGHBOY AFRAID OF?
READ
בן & ג'רי'ס
1987
This is the year Ben & Jerry's opens in Canada and Israel. (The Israeli T-shirts read from right to left.)
1986
A new flavor is born—CHERRY GARCIA! It's their third most popular flavor—Ta da!
STILL 1986
n & Jerry's
pens its new
e cream factory
Waterbury,
ermont. They
ve tours... and
ee samples, too.
Meanwhile, in Cleveland, Ohio Cowmobile burns up, creating the world's biggest Baked Alaska.

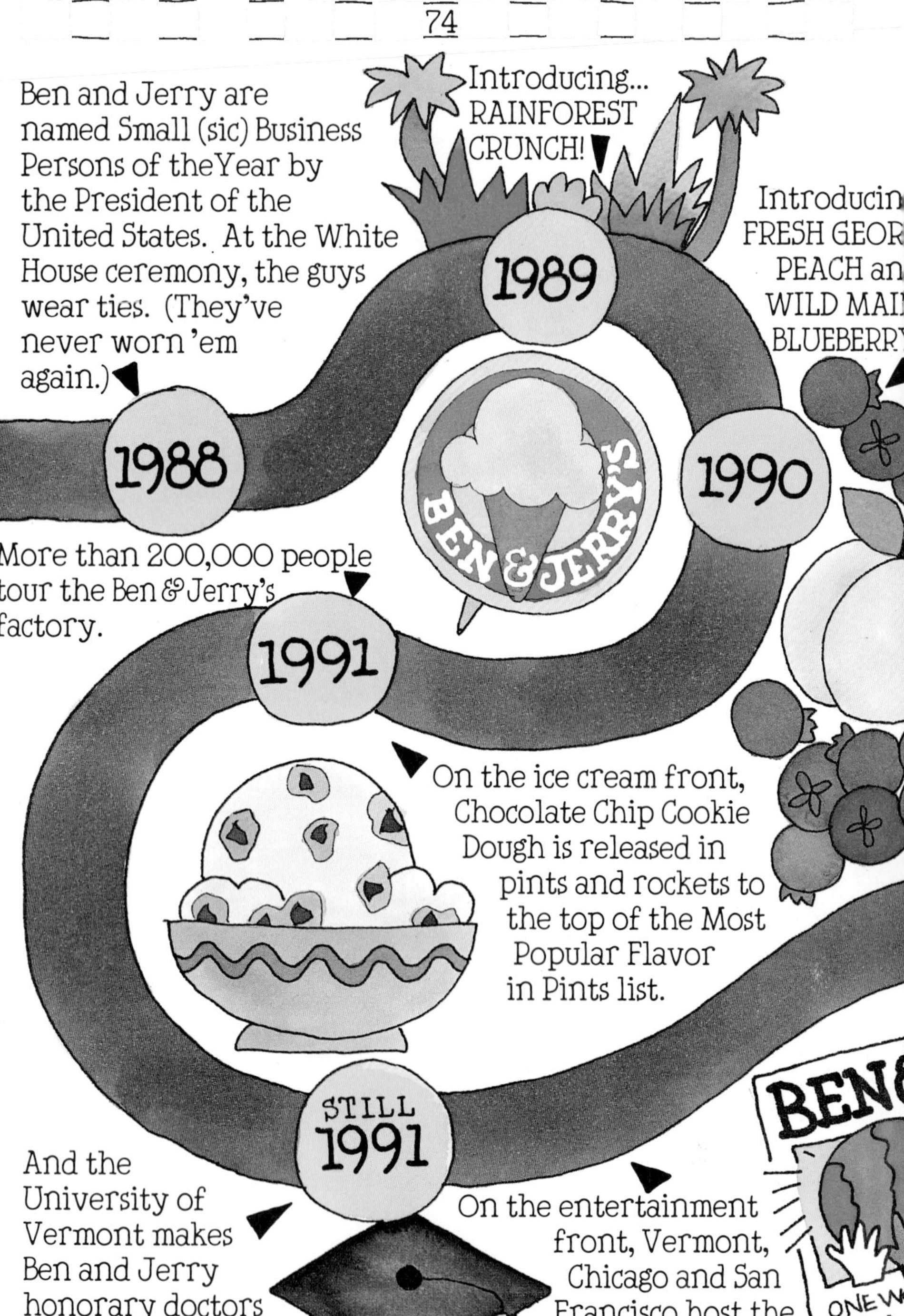
Ben and Jerry are named Small (sic) Business Persons of the Year by the President of the United States. At the White House ceremony, the guys wear ties. (They've never worn 'em again.)
1988
Introducing... RAINFOREST CRUNCH!
1989
Introducin
FRESH GEOR
PEACH an
WILD MAI
BLUEBERR
1990
BEN & JERRY'S
More than 200,000 people tour the Ben & Jerry's factory.
1991
On the ice cream front, Chocolate Chip Cookie Dough is released in pints and rockets to the top of the Most Popular Flavor in Pints list.
STILL 1991
And the University of Vermont makes Ben and Jerry honorary doctors of law. The crowd gives them a standing ovation.
On the entertainment front, Vermont, Chicago and San Francisco host the first One World, One Heart Festivals.
BEN
ONE W
FE

Building starts on the third Ben & Jerry's ice cream factory, in St. Albans, Vermont.

1992's big new flavor is WAVY GRAVY.

And the one-millionth visitor takes the factory tour in Waterbury. (His name is Mr. Woo, and he got free T-shirts, free hats and a year's supply of free ice cream.)

he farm
it, Ben & Jerry's
farmers extra
their milk at a time
n farmers are losing their
ts–and sometimes their farms!.

The first Scoop Shop opens in Russia!

And, the first Scoop Shop opens in Harlem! Three-quarters of the Harlem store's profits go to Hark Homes Men's Shelter.

EVERY FLAVOR WE CAN REMEMBER

check off the flavors you have tried!

- ❑ Cherry Garcia®
- ❑ Chunky Monkey®
- ❑ Dastardly Mash®
- ❑ Vanilla
- ❑ Heath® Bar Crunch
- ❑ Mint with Oreo® Cookies
- ❑ New York Super Fudge Chunk
- ❑ Vanilla Chocolate Chunk
- ❑ White Russian™
- ❑ Strawberry
- ❑ Coffee Heath® Bar Crunch
- ❑ Raspberry
- ❑ Chocolate Almond
- ❑ Chocolate Chocolate Chip
- ❑ Sweet Cream with Oreo® Cookies
- ❑ Chocolate Cointreau® Orange Fudge
- ❑ Chocolate
- ❑ Coffee
- ❑ Mint Chocolate Chunk
- ❑ Orange Cream
- ❑ Apple Pie
- ❑ Butter Pecan
- ❑ Maple Walnut
- ❑ Chocolate Fudge Brownie
- ❑ Chocolate Raspberry Swirl
- ❑ Chocolate Swiss Chocolate Almond
- ❑ Banana Strawberry
- ❑ Chocolate Chip Cookie Dough
- ❑ Kaffaretto™
- ❑ Miller Family Malt
- ❑ Mocha Chunk
- ❑ Karelia Krunch
- ❑ Mint Chocolate Cookie
- ❑ Lemon Peppermint Carob Chip
- ❑ Peanut Butter Chocolate Chunk
- ❑ Peanut Butter Cup
- ❑ Pistachio Pistachio
- ❑ Mandarin Chocolate
- ❑ Miz Jelena's Sweet Potato Pie
- ❑ Praline Pecan
- ❑ Rainforest Crunch™
- ❑ Reverse Chocolate Chunk
- ❑ Vanilla Swiss Chocolate Almond
- ❑ Chocolate Fudge
- ❑ French Vanilla
- ❑ Nutcracker Suite
- ❑ Mocha Walnut
- ❑ Egg Nog
- ❑ Chocolate Heath® Bar Crunch
- ❑ Sweet Cream with Cookies
- ❑ Coconut Milk Chocolate Almond
- ❑ Cinnamon
- ❑ Ethan Almond
- ❑ Mocha Swiss Chocolate Almond
- ❑ Vanilla M&M®
- ❑ Chocolate Gingersnap
- ❑ Cappuccino
- ❑ Chocolate Mystic Mint®
- ❑ Chocolate Hazelnut Swirl
- ❑ Tennessee Mud with Jack Daniel's®
- ❑ Sambuca® Coffee Flake
- ❑ Rachel's Brownies®
- ❑ Macadamia Nut
- ❑ Sugar Plum
- ❑ Tuskegee Chunk
- ❑ Wild Maine Blueberry
- ❑ Fresh Georgia Peach
- ❑ Vanilla Fudge Swirl
- ❑ Blueberry Cheesecake
- ❑ Coffee Almond Fudge
- ❑ Honey Vanilla
- ❑ Amanda Brulée
- ❑ Maple Grape-Nut®
- ❑ Gingersnap
- ❑ Banana
- ❑ Grape-Nut®
- ❑ Cantaloupe
- ❑ Peanut Butter
- ❑ Honey Apple Raisin Walnut
- ❑ Cappuccino Chip
- ❑ Wavy Gravy

OR: HOW TO MAKE ICE CREAM AND HAVE FUN!

Ice Cream ingredients you will need:

1 cup milk
1 cup heavy cream
1/2 cup sugar
1 egg
1 teaspoon vanilla extract

Ice Cream-making things you will need:

1. One 1-pound size can with a cover (coffee cans are good).
2. One larger container (preferably sturdy plastic) with cover. Should be large enough to hold the smaller can plus ice.
3. Ice (at least a 2-gallon bucket of small cubes).
4. Rock salt (1 bag--you can find it at grocery stores and hardware stores).
5. Mixing bowl
6. Egg beater or whisk
7. Tape (the heavy-duty kind, like duct tape)

Mix all the ingredients thoroughly with an egg beater or whisk. Pour the mixture into the smaller can and secure the cover with tape. Place the smaller can into the larger container and add a layer of ice and a layer of rock salt until the container is full. the cover of the large container with tape, if necessary.

Gather friends or classmates around, sit in a large circle on the floor, and begin to roll the container from person to person across the circle. Roll the container for 10-15 minutes, then refill with salt and ice as necessary. Continue rolling for another 10-15 minutes (you may have to repeat this step if your ice cream's not quite ready), then open up the inner container and VOILA!, it's Vanilla ice cream for you all to share and enjoy!

Optional: Create your own ice cream original -- add your choice of fun CHUNKS (candies, cookies, fruits, even gummy worms!) to your mixture after your first 10-15 minutes of rolling.

Ooh, the possibilities!

HOW I CAN...

Take the Ben & Jerry's

FACTORY TOUR...

1. Ride, bike, hike or paddle to Waterbury, Vermont, any day of the week.
2. Bring a dollar for every adult (50 cents goes to Vermont Community groups). Kids get in FREE.
3. Call the TOUR HOTLINE for late-breaking news. The number is (802) 244-TOUR.
4. If you're bringing a gazillion people, call (802)244-5641 before you show up. Please.

to Ben and Jerry . . .

1. Address your letter to: Ben & Jerry
P. O. Box 240
Waterbury, Vermont 05676
2. Tell 'em Jules says Hi!

Get Ben & Jerry's

CHUNK MAIL

1. Find a postcard.
2. Write your name, address, city, state and zip code on it.
3. Mail it to: Ben & Jerry's Chunk Mail
P. O. Box 240
Waterbury, Vermont 05676